UKLA

The United Kingdom Literacy Association
formerly The United Kingdom Reading Association

REVISED EDITION

Tell Me Another...
Speaking, Listening and Learning Through Storytelling

By Jacqueline Harrett

Minibook 28

UKLA Minibook Series

Series Editor Eve Bearne
Past Editors Alison B. Littlefair, Bobbie Neate, Ros Fisher, Susan Ellis

Minibooks in print

Developing Narrative Writing 7-13	Roy Corden
Children's Writing Journals	Lynda Graham and Annette Johnson
Drama: Reading, Writing and Speaking Our Way Forward	Teresa Grainger and Angela Pickard
Literature Circles: Better Talking, More Ideas	Carole King and Jane Briggs
Making Reading Mean	Vivienne Smith
Storyline - Promoting Language Across the Curriculum	Steve Bell and Sallie Harkness
Miscue Analysis in the Classroom (revised second edition)	Robin Campbell
Classroom Action Research in Literacy: a Guide to Practice	Eve Bearne, Lynda Graham and Jackie Marsh
Active encounters: Inspiring young readers and writers of non-fiction 4-11	Margaret Mallett
Poetry Matters (revised second edition)	Andrew Lambirth
Dyslexia and Inclusion: supporting classroom reading with 7-11 year olds	Rosemary Anderson
Practical Bilingual Strategies for Multilingual Classrooms	Tözün Issa and Alayne Öztürk

Issue number 28
Tell Me Another... Speaking, Listening and Learning Through Storytelling
by Jacqueline Harrett

First published 2004 2nd edition 2009
ISBN 978 1 897638 49 1

UKLA is willing to allow UKLA members to make multiple copies of up to 10% of this work for distribution within an educational institution or a local authority. Permission need not be sought for such copying.

Published by UKLA
United Kingdom Literacy Association,
4th Floor, Attenborough Building, University of Leicester LE1 7RH
www.ukla.org

The United Kingdom Reading Association (UKRA) became the United Kingdom Literacy Association (UKLA) on May 25th 2003 © United Kingdom Literacy Association

Tell Me Another...
Speaking, Listening and Learning Through Storytelling

Contents

Introduction	The Power of stories	1
	Storytelling	2
	Listening differently	3
	Storytelling and the curriculum	5
Chapter 1	Storytelling - getting started	7
	Choice of story	7
	Remembering	9
	Teaching children to become storytellers	10
	Using the skeleton	13
	Story beginnings	13
	Story endings	14
Chapter 2	Using traditional stories	15
	Rhiannon Goch - a retelling of *Red Riding Hood*	17
Chapter 3	Historical contexts	22
	Practical application	22
	The children's responses	24
	What the children learned about history	25
	The views of the teachers	28
Chapter 4	Storytelling and writing	29
	Wanting to write in a reception class	29
	Examples from a reception class	30
	Personal narrative	31
	Passing on the story	32
	Embellishments	32
	Description	32
	Dialogue	34
	Emotion	36
	Conclusion	39
	References	40
	Further Reading	43
	Resources	44

Dedications:

For my parents, Andrew and Norah Montgomery, who gave me a childhood filled with love, laughter and stories.

Thanks:

My grateful thanks to the following schools:

Glyn Coed Infant and Nursery School
Howell's Junior School
Roath Park Primary School
Bryn Celyn Primary School

Introduction

The Power of stories

Stories, like dreams, take us to places we have never seen, activities we have never experienced, events we have not witnessed and introduces us to people we have not met. Through narrative we escape the everyday, the mundane, and travel to a land of new experiences. We can explore danger and fear from the comfort of knowing that it is fantasy and not reality. This mental journey, which most people would describe as imagination, needs to be developed in children and storytelling is one way to do so. Narrative is 'central to early learning and thinking' across the curriculum (Grainger, 1997). Oral storytelling develops the visualisation skills that aid memory and enhance understanding and encourages development of speaking and listening skills.

Oral storytelling also seems to be becoming marginalized in schools. The pressures of a narrow curriculum may be blamed in part for this (Winston & Tandy, 2001). Teachers make comments like:

> I haven't got time.
> We have to use the time for reading.
> I'd like to do more storytelling and the children enjoy it but is it really educational?

This last response is, I suspect, what a great majority of teachers feel because 'The value in terms of literacy is not so instantly visible' (Graham and Kelly, 2000:72). Storytelling seems to be almost a subversive act and the benefits difficult to measure while 'teaching pertains to what is real and knowable' (Paley, 1995:3). With increasing pressure on teachers to produce evidence of learning how do they prove that storytelling is beneficial?

The complexity of the fundamental skills of speaking and listening can often be lost in the current emphasis on reading and writing. Effective oral communication is at the basis of our society and without this skill children are at a disadvantage. It seems extraordinary that oracy is almost a sleeping partner in the literacy process or, as Alexander believes, 'at best a poor relation' in Britain (2002). The Independent Review of the Primary Curriculum acknowledges this by admitting that 'discussion of reading, writing and numeracy in primary education often fails to recognize the central importance of developing children's spoken communication' (Rose, 2008:3). The renewed Primary Framework in England emphasises the role of speaking and listening in language and communication development and all of the suggestions in this book fulfil the objectives in the speaking and listening strands (see: http://nationalstrategies.standards.dcsf.gov.uk/strands/ accessed 3rd March 2009).

Through the telling and retelling of stories children develop effective communication and also self-confidence. Storytelling encourages active listening and audience response and allows the child to extend and explore narrative in a unique and personal way. Baker and Greene (1977) advocate the use of oral stories for many reasons including supporting the curriculum and preserving cultural heritage. In our multicultural society this is important if all children are to feel valued. What better way to celebrate cultural differences than by telling stories from around the world? This can involve parents re-telling the stories from their childhoods to their children who, in turn, can share with others in the class. My personal introduction into storytelling was through my parents during my childhood in Ireland. My mother constantly recounted everyday anecdotes in detail and my father coloured my childhood with tales of fairies, giants and 'the little people'. It was pure magic and I was lost in the world of the imagination.

Storytelling

Storytelling is often used as a blanket term to cover the areas of both oral stories and their written counterparts. Writers are described as good story-tellers when what is meant is that they are able to write a story convincingly. Although the oral and the written are intertwined in many ways it is important to make a distinction between the two discrete forms of storytelling and story-reading.

Grugeon and Gardner's (2000) comment on the difference between written and oral stories is worth reflecting upon:

Perhaps that is the difference between reading and telling; reading is a process of sharing and interpreting a text that someone else has produced but telling a story is a unique and personal performance (Grugeon and Gardner, 2000: 2).

Mallan (1991) deliberates at length on the differences between the two modes of story and says:

With storytelling, the interaction is creative, as both teller and listener create the story. Words are used to create mental pictures of the story. The storyteller's face, voice, body and personality help to convey meaning and mood. During story reading both listener and reader are conscious of the book (Mallan, 1991: 5).

The uniqueness of the oral story is reflected upon and the interaction between the teller and the listeners is seen as an important, and indeed essential, element of this uniqueness. Mallan (1991) comments on the mental images created through the words but it is not simply the words but the manner in which the words are transferred which is important to 'meaning and mood.'

Listening differently

Bearne (2000) maintains that the challenge in schools today is not so much to develop children's listening skills as to develop their awareness of how to pay attention. Involving children in meaningful and interesting listening activities to maintain attention is important. Baker and Greene (1977) argue that storytelling encourages the art of listening as a storytelling session presupposes listeners who play an active part in the process. Listening to and sharing stories also enables children to develop their vocabulary in a meaningful and pleasurable way (Browne, 2007).

In my experience of teaching young children I have noticed that children listen in different ways and I have categorised these into different groups. Teachers will undoubtedly recognise pupils under the different categories:

- *Participatory:* these are the children who play a part in oral sessions, joining in refrains and actions and showing an active role in the process. They are fully engaged, eyes fixed on the speaker and openly reacting and interacting with the story or activity.

- **Reflective:** these children listen but can appear to take a more passive approach. Although they remain fixed on the words and actions of the activity their responses are less obvious. They may just smile or nod in reaction to a part of a story and it is difficult to gauge their thoughts.
- **Superficial:** children who appear to be listening but who are not fully attentive. They may be quiet and look as if they are aware of everything but in fact they are just hearing the words without reviewing or thinking about what is being said.
- **Deceptive:** listeners who appear to be inattentive but who are able to recall the story, or what was said, in detail. Sometimes these children will seem to be more interested in the Velcro on their shoes, the books or toys on the shelf or even the jumper or hair of the child nearest to them yet they can tell you exactly what has been said.
- **Inattentive:** the child who has heard but not listened actively and is unable to recall anything but the very basics of what has been spoken. These listeners may display symptoms of superficial or deceptive listening. Some children look as if they are listening (superficial) but are not. Others (deceptive) are obviously not paying full attention. It is only through talking to the children that the teacher can estimate how much they have actively listened and into which category the child fits.

As teachers we want to encourage children to listen rather than just hear. Oral storytelling often succeeds in producing more active listeners, possibly because it appeals to a wider range of learning styles. Storytelling is a performance art, a mode of delivery that invites active listening. It demands reaction and interaction and participation from the audience as it depends very much on the use of voice, gesture and eye contact. It is a shared experience and through active listening the audience is transported to a different world.

Storytelling and the curriculum

Baker and Greene (1977) advocate the use of oral stories for many reasons: interpretations of life; to create inward images; to please the ear and encourage listening skills; to support the curriculum; to preserve cultural heritage and to give 'dramatic joy' to children and ourselves. The justification for storytelling is apparent but a tension still exists between the demands of the curriculum and what is perceived as a playful aspect of the curriculum. Teachers find it difficult to deal with the lack of evidence that oral work involves (Howe: 1997). It is ephemeral, difficult to capture and difficult to assess. If oral stories are used in the classroom, some teachers believe they need to have a written follow-up to prove the benefit, so emphasis in school shifts to the skills of reading and writing. Although one section in this book refers to storytelling as a precursor for writing it comes with a health warning. A good story can be spoilt and the learning eroded if too much emphasis is placed on a written end product. With storytelling the process is as important, if not more so, than the product. Children need to gain confidence in their ability to communicate orally without the pressure of writing afterwards. They need to be aware that the spoken word is valuable and their attempts at telling stories are valued, regardless of the fact that they are possibly unstructured or hesitant. Everyone learns a new skill through practice and the only way children, and teachers, will become expert is through practice and endless opportunities to explore oral narrative.

For young children, talking is the way they organise their thoughts and make sense of the world about them. Even as adults we all use narrative to explain everyday events; indeed, contextualising matters into narrative form often helps us to understand difficult concepts or traumatic events. Oral communication is still central to our society and storytelling is at the basis of our culture.

> *…it really makes them listen. They pay more attention when I tell them a story so I use storytelling a lot.* (Year 1 teacher)

This particular teacher has found the benefits of storytelling and, while fulfilling the curriculum, has given it an added dimension by skilful use of oral story. Student teachers also gain in confidence after engaging in this type of interchange with pupils and soon value what, at first, seems like a great deal of extra work.

I'd never done that before (told a story) but it was really good and they really listened. (Student teacher)

In this book I wish to explore three areas: traditional stories, historical contexts and storytelling into writing. These are areas where I feel that storytelling has definite advantages and helps fulfill the demands of the curriculum while engaging pupils and encouraging them to listen actively and think about what they have heard.

Chapter 1

Storytelling - getting started

Colwell (1988) lists the qualities of a good storyteller:
- Creative imagination
- A feeling for drama and skill in portraying
- A capacity for humour
- A wide knowledge of books
- Belief in the value of telling stories

If that list seems rather daunting it is not meant to be. The most important point is probably the last one because a belief in telling stories will overcome any difficulties. Thinking back to childhood many people had a parent, grandparent or other relative who made them laugh by recounting everyday incidents in a dramatic fashion. That was storytelling, but of a different kind, and it is something we all do everyday. What happens when someone goes home after the day's work? Nine times out of ten they probably recount, in detail, the problems or funny incidents of the day. They make sense of the day and rid themselves of frustrations by sharing the story with family and friends. As Colwell (1980) and Meek (1991) point out, we are all storytellers to some degree, although to tell a story properly and with conviction needs time and practice. (Graves, 1990; Graham and Kelly, 2000) What follows is a number of aspects that are important when learning how to use storytelling in the classroom.

Choice of story

The first ingredient is the story. The choice of story is very important. It should be a story with a strong storyline. Stories from folklore and those stemming from the oral tradition are the type of stories that are usually successful and easy to learn. Different countries have their own stories so this is an ideal way of extending understanding of different cultures. The cultural diversity in our schools is growing and we need to embrace the differences and extend our knowledge of other cultures. Story is one way to do this.

The stories also need to appeal to the chosen audience and have a visual impact. Teachers know the needs of their class and can make balanced judgements based on knowledge about the types of stories that will appeal to the children. A class of Year 6, mainly boys, is hardly likely to be interested in tales of fluffy bunnies. Children are surprisingly bloodthirsty in the stories they enjoy listening to and retelling. As Fox (1993) found out they are not interested in the dull and 'sanitised'. Traditional fairy stories, legends, myths and folklore stem from the oral tradition and are suitable for any age although preparation is vital, as the story may have to be modified to suit the age group.

Anyone venturing down the oral storytelling path for the first time would do well to start with a story they are familiar with, enjoy, and can tell in their own way. Once they have achieved success they can widen their repertoire.

Some stories to try

Year 2	Year 5/6
The Owl and the Woodpecker and *Hunter and his Dog* by Brian Wildsmith : OUP *What made Tiddalik Laugh?* by Joanna Troughton : Puffin *Rainbow Bird* and *The Fire Children* by Eric Maddern : Frances Lincoln	*Tales for the Telling* by Edna O'Brien : Pavilion Books *King Arthur Stories* by Rosemary Sutcliff : Red Fox *Myths and Legends* retold by Anthony Horowitz : Kingfisher

Remembering

For those teachers who are used to storytelling, the task of learning how to tell a story is not a problem. They will have devised their own system for 'learning' the story. For others it may seem a frightening task to leave behind the comfort of the known (story-reading) and delve into the unknown (storytelling). Sometimes people are afraid that they will forget the story and be unable to continue but what must be remembered is that the teller has ownership of the tale. If a detail is forgotten or something needs to be changed to suit the audience then this can be done without anyone knowing the original intention. It leaves the storyteller in a uniquely strong position. We do not need to rehearse the details of what happened during the day before going home to tell the family. The mundane everyday events of our lives are interpreted by our thoughts and embellished in the telling.

Ways to remember a story vary from person to person. One of the best ways of remembering a story is to tell it over and over again until it is part the subconscious memory. Some storytellers depend on keeping a type of cinematic viewpoint in their minds while others like to map the main points out or draw pictures and diagrams. Whatever your preferred memory technique it is always a good idea to identify the main events in a story as the points of reference. When teaching children to tell and retell stories this is essential. By recapping and sequencing the story framework, you help them to remember and visualise these important staging posts in the story.

Some storytellers like to use props to help them remember the sequence of events in a story. Props can range from a puppet to the storytelling apron, bag or coat from which various objects connected to the story are produced during the telling. Prompt cards with drawings of the main events may be turned over at the appropriate times during the telling of a story. It is even possible to hang objects or cards from a string, like a washing line, as a visual reminder for children to develop and invent their own stories. Although all these items have their uses it must be remembered that the main attributes of a storyteller are voice, eye contact and gesture. Props can be useful but they can also detract from the main purpose of the exercise, which is to involve the audience to become *participatory* or *reflective* listeners. Children who are lost in story sit quietly with eyes, and mouths, open when actively listening to the tale unfold.

Teaching children to become storytellers

Sharing a story skeleton with children and working together to identify which events are really important, because they are central to the story, is a significant task to be undertaken as a whole class. A story skeleton is simply a short plan, frame or *aide memoire* to help sequence the main events in a story. Once children have the basics they are free to elaborate and embellish as much as they wish. In fact this is to be encouraged as by adding to the story skeleton they are inventing and using their imaginations to produce unique and creative stories, entirely of their own construction. The purpose of a story skeleton, or plan, is to show the sequence of events. It is a guide, not a straightjacket, and children must be aware that it is meant as an aid and not as the entire plan.

Introducing the idea of a story skeleton to the children is easy. The diagram in Figure 1 shows a simple format. The teacher scribes as the children recount the significant events of the story. The skeleton is confined to six lines to maintain conciseness and the teacher can demonstrate the use of note form rather than using complicated sentences. Picture clues may be added to each line to remind the less confident or younger children of the key points. This exercise in itself is useful for children as it could also be used as a plan for writing.

Skeletons may be in different formats such as a type of storyboard, grid or diagram. Children can be introduced to different ways of remembering and noting key events and then they may choose their preferred format, as in Figures 2.0, 2.1, 2.2 and 2.3.

Figure 1 Example of a story skeleton for *Cinderella*.

Year 6 Story skeletons showing different ways of planning

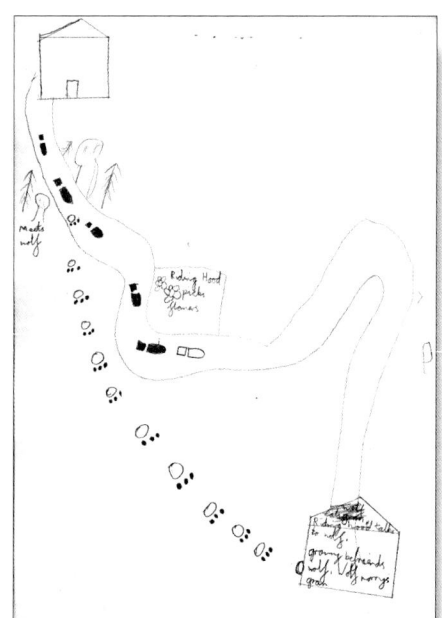

Figure 2.0   Figure 2.1

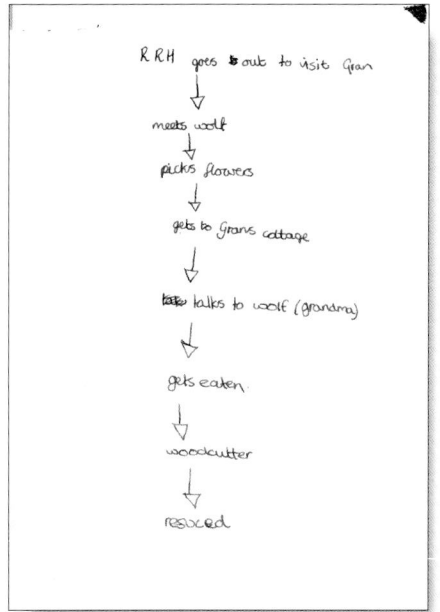

Figure 2.2   Figure 2.3

Using the Skeleton

Deviation from the story skeleton should be applauded as this indicates imaginative response and shows confidence and creativity. Introducing the 'what if?' factor is often how writers find their inspiration and asking open questions such as, 'I wonder what would have happened if Cinderella's fairy godmother mixed up her spells?' or 'What if Grandma fought the wolf and frightened him?' is one way to encourage children to think creatively. Permitting children to deviate from the norm ought to be encouraged. Ian, a Year 1 child, obsessed with dinosaurs, retold the story of Tiddalik the frog. Halfway through the retelling he decided that Jurassic Park was a better story and proceeded to weave the film into his recount. It made a very interesting if rather bizarre story, but demonstrated vast oral competence, imagination and self-confidence. It also illustrated the strong influence of the media in the lives of children of the twenty first century. This influence of the media is demonstrated clearly in the reports by Bearne *et al.* on research conducted by UKLA with the QCA (UKLA /QCA, 2004, 2005; Bearne *et al.*, 2007).

Story beginnings

Imagine that the story has been chosen and learnt (not by rote as this spoils the spontaneity) and the novice storyteller is about to begin. Many storytellers have signals that they use to convey the start of a story. They may play a drum or other musical instrument, rattle a rain stick or basket of stones and shells, hum or just sit perfectly still to indicate the story-telling is about to start. In the Caribbean the procedure is to shout 'cric crac' to the audience who must respond in the same way. This ensures that the audience is focused in the beginning and gives a clear indication that the story is about to begin and that the audience are to play a major part in the telling by listening actively and participating in the telling of the story. The signal given is the choice of the teller and unique to that person. Some people feel that they need a prop, such as a bell or a chant while others will simply hum or begin their tale with a familiar phrase such as 'One day a long time ago…'.

Story endings

In a similar fashion, the end of a story may be signalled by the same musical tone, sign or phrase. This gives a clear indication that the story has finished and the teller will say no more. Young children often finish with a satisfied 'And that's the end'. Often the end of a story is greeted by silence, which is something novice storytellers may find unnerving. This silence, however, is simply indicating that the listeners have absorbed the story and they are bringing themselves back from fantasy to reality. Occasionally the end of a story is met by a universal sigh. Far from indicating disillusionment, this is a symptom of involvement with the fantasy world to such a degree that the participants, the listeners, have difficulty extraditing themselves from the fantasy world they have become so involved in. Think what it is like when you go to the cinema and see an absorbing film. At the end you feel you almost have to drag yourself back to reality. You may feel the same after reading a good book and scenes from the story will be replaying in your mind for hours, sometimes days. Storytelling allows for different learning styles as it engages not just the aural but also the visual. If the storyteller incorporates actions into the telling it also appeals to the kinaesthetic learner. This variety of modes ensures all members of the class are involved.

Chapter 2

Using traditional stories

Using traditional stories and giving them a twist, or a different perspective, is one way to encourage children to listen carefully. If they are familiar with the stories from the dominant culture, or their own culture, then these may be changed and adapted to give a different slant. Consider how the story of *The Gingerbread Man* is similar to the tale of *The Runaway Chapatti*. In essence it is the same story but it has a different setting and the main character, the chapatti, makes it more accessible to Asian children as it reflects their home experiences. The changes provide a new version of the same story that will appeal to a wider and more multicultural audience. As our society becomes a melting pot of different races and cultures we need to represent all these different cultures in our storytelling.

Many stories have similar roots and may be traced across continents. The story of creation, for example, may be based in the Bible and the Qur'an but also has different versions, such as *The Fire Children* (Maddern: 1993) from other cultures. One of our most familiar fairy stories, *Red Riding Hood*, stems from a French story, *le Petit Chaperon Rouge*, published by Perrault in 1697. It is likely this came from an oral tale from South France and Northern Italy. According to Zipes (1991) in Perrault's version the girl, of sinful nature, meets the wolf and makes a wager with him to see who will arrive at the grandmother's house first. The wolf arrives first, devours the grandmother and takes her place in bed. The girl arrives, gets into bed and asks the wolf questions about his unusual appearance before being eaten by him. In 1812 the brothers Grimm added their own variations and since then many versions have been written and told throughout the world. Versions of stories on audio or video are also available for discussion and may be used in the narrative strand of the Literacy Framework in England.

In Wales there is a requirement to fulfil the curriculum Cymreig which means that the unique culture and language of Wales must be highlighted at every opportunity. Many other parts of England, Scotland and Ireland have a similar desire to preserve distinct regional languages, dialects and identities. One way to meet this common requirement is to tell stories but to give them a setting particular to the region. In Wales, using geographical and linguistic features in the story not only highlights the curriculum Cymreig but also makes children aware of different versions. The story *Rhiannon Goch*, which follows, is a written version of the *Red Riding Hood* story. I have told this version many times to children in different schools in Wales but always had the same response. *'That's Red Riding Hood,'* shouted Rhys, as soon as I had finished telling the story. Even four year olds are able to recognise common threads. Immediately the children started talking about how they had books with the story and the similarities and differences in their picture book versions and the story they had just heard. The children had not just heard the story but had listened actively and were responding appropriately to the version of the story they had heard.

RHIANNON GOCH
A retelling of *Red Riding Hood*

Once upon a time, a long time ago, there lived a little girl called Rhiannon. She lived in the middle of Wales and everyone around called her Rhiannon Goch because of her long red curly hair.

One day her Mam said, 'Rhiannon Bach, Mamgu is ill and I want you to take this basket over to her and stay with her until Tadgu finishes cutting wood in the forest. I've put in some cawl, bara and menyn, a piece of teisen and some of my home made toffi. It'll help her sore throat. Go through the forest but stay on the path and make sure you don't talk to anyone on the way.'

Rhiannon put on her boots and her cosy red cardigan and set off through the dark forest. She hurried along and was nearly at the end of the forest when a huge grey hairy wolf leapt from behind a tree.

'Bore da,' he said, smiling and showing his yellow fanged teeth. 'Where are you going and what have you got in that basket? Something smells hyfryd.'

Rhiannon remembered what her Mam had said about talking to strangers but the wolf was standing directly in front of her so she had no choice but to answer.

'Well, there's some cawl, bara and teisen for my Mamgu. She's not very well.'

'Where does Mamgu live?'

'Just over there in the cottage at the other side of the forest. You can see the smoke from the chimney if you look.'

The wolf looked. 'Indeed you can. You'd better run along then.'

Rhiannon breathed a sigh of relief and almost ran out of the forest. When she reached the bright sunshine at the other side of the trees she could see a wonderful sight. In front of her, all around were hundreds of beautiful yellow daffodils. 'Oh!' exclaimed Rhiannon, 'Mamgu would love some of these.' And stopping to put down her basket she picked a bunch of the pretty flowers.

Meanwhile the wolf had run to the cottage and knocked on the door.

'Dewch i mewn,' croaked Mamgu, thinking it was Rhiannon. When she saw the wolf she screamed and ran and hid in the wardrobe.

The wolf grabbed a shawl and Mamgu's bonnet and had just jumped into the still-warm bed when Rhiannon arrived. She thought it strange that the door was open but came into the cottage nevertheless.

'Mamgu. It's Rhiannon Goch. I've brought you some things to eat.'

'Bring it here, cariad,' replied the wolf, in what he hoped was his sweetest voice.

Rhiannon took the basket over to the bed. 'And look Mamgu at the lovely daffodils I picked for you. Smell how sweet they are.'

Rhiannon pushed the flowers towards the wolf's nose.

'Oh Mamgu. What a big nose you've got.'

'All the better to smell the flowers with cariad.'

'I'll put them in some water and put the cawl on to boil,' said Rhiannon, going over to the open fire and putting the pot of soup on to the ring above.

'Come and talk to me cariad,' begged the wolf, licking his lips at the sight of Rhiannon's plump little arms. He stretched out a paw.

'Oh Mamgu, how hairy your hands are.'

'All the better to stroke you with cariad,' and the wolf laid one huge hairy paw on Rhiannon's shoulder. Rhiannon's heart missed a beat but she was a clever little girl and did not show how frightened she was.

'Let me put some menyn on your sore hands Mamgu,' she said rubbing the butter all over the wolf's paws.

The wolf growled a little and opened his mouth wide.

'Oh Mamgu what big teeth you've got!' cried Rhiannon. 'Here have some toffi,' and before the wolf could say, 'All the better to eat you with cariad' he found his mouth so full of toffi that his teeth were stuck together. This made him furious and with a deep growl he leapt out of the bed. Rhainnon ran to the fire and lifted the pot of steaming cawl. The wolf landed at her feet but his paws were so slippery with the menyn that he slid into the fire. Rhiannon threw the pot of cawl over his head and with a great howl of pain he disappeared through the door just as Tadgu was returning.

Mamgu opened the wardrobe door and cried with relief when she saw Rhiannon and Tadgu. They did not have cawl for lunch but they ate the rest of the fresh-baked bara and teisin and laughed at their lucky escape.

And the wolf? Well, the last they heard of him he was heading straight for Anglesey and he was never seen in the forest again.

Teachers can use this story to help children invent heir own versions, unique to their local community. Use of local dialect also highlights Standard English and the story may be set in any country or region so personalising it and making it relevant to the children of that area. Begin by identifying key words and placing the story in a familiar setting. Perhaps there is a wood close to the school or a park that may have a copse of trees suitable for hiding a wolf. In the inner city children may be able to identify for themselves an area where frightening creatures may live - 'the urban jungle'.

This is one example of how traditional stories can be twisted and added to, giving a personal appeal to children and widening their perceptions of story. They realise that what is written may be changed in the telling and that orally they are the masters of the game. Children can take traditional stories from their own cultures and identify key features that can be changed or added to and do whatever they want to make the story their own. Their story is unique and may be adjusted as many times as necessary as long as the essence remains the same. *Cinderella* may be set in Bangladesh, Jamaica or Iceland just as easily as anywhere else. Indeed, many of our popular films are re-tellings of themes that occur in these traditional tales. *Maid in Manhattan*, (2003) for example, is a film version of the *Cinderella* story. Children should be able to realise that in the oral re-telling of stories they are masters. It encourages children to explore the nature and rhythm of narrative and is empowering; no-one can say they are wrong.

Key Words for *Rhiannon Goch*

Goch	red (mutation of coch)	**Menyn**	butter
Mam	Mum	**Teisen**	cake
Mamgu	Grandma	**Toffi**	toffee
Tadgu	Grandad	**Bore da**	Good morning
Cawl	soup	**Hyfryd**	lovely
Bara	bread	**Dewch I mewn**	Come in
		Cariad	darling

Figure 3.0

Figure 3.1

Chapter 3

Historical Contexts

Storytelling should not just be confined to a slot in the literacy curriculum. It is cross-curricular in nature and can add an extra dimension to all subjects. Shaw and Hawes (1998) recommend storytelling and the use of metaphor as a 'brain-friendly' way of learning. Turner-Bisset (2001) has also used storytelling to enhance history lessons and regards it as 'of central importance: …, and as a way of engaging the children's imaginations' (Turner-Bisset, 2001: 27). Rubright (1996) equally sees story in its many guises as being at the heart of the curriculum no matter what the content of the subject area. The *Independent Review of the Primary Curriculum* (Rose, 2008) aims to develop a way of ensuring that subject areas and cross-curricular working are not seen as polar opposites. Using storytelling in historical contexts enables both literacy and history to be developed in tandem and follows the recommendations of the review to realise the potential of role play and drama for language development.

The following ideas for the history curriculum came from Gillard (1996). In a workshop activity Gillard gave groups a few pages each from the life history of a person and asked them to provide a first-draft retelling. The facts were pieced together to give an overview of the life of that person.

Practical application

I replicated this idea with a class of Year 5 children. I spent a morning with the children and worked with them, in conjunction with the class teacher, to retell the life of Henry VIII in storytelling format. They had just completed a history project on Tudors and Stuarts so had prior knowledge of the facts, an aspect that was important in the success of the session. The class was divided into four groups, each of whom had a pack with information about one period of Henry's life.

PACK A	**PACK B**
Information about Catherine of Aragon, including a portrait	Information about Anne Boleyn
A letter from Sarah Wiseman (1564)	Letter from Anne to Henry begging for mercy and speech at her execution
Details about food in Tudor times	Information about the church and the Reformation
Pictures of a Tudor house	Illustrations and descriptions of childhood in Tudor times

PACK C	**PACK D**
Information about Jane Seymour and Anne of Cleves	Information about Catherine Howard and Catherine Parr
Information about printing and painting and music	Information about ships and dress in Tudor times
Copy of *Pastime with Good Company (The King's Ballad)*	Picture of Tudor dress and Henry's armour

(Sources for these packs are in the final section of the book.)

The only provisos were that they met the deadline for having their story ready for delivery to the rest of the class and that they had to have a storyteller. They were free to organise themselves in whatever form they wished and add drama, freeze frame, mime or what ever other device they thought was appropriate. Simple costumes were provided for the children to use, if they wished, and these seemed to be popular as a signal for the role-play activities that followed. Donning a costume seemed to help the children to lose any inhibitions and to take on the persona of their character. This seems to illustrate the need for 'play' activities with juniors. Too often the enjoyment is taken from learning by the serious way it is presented. Role-play is essential, for all children and possibly more so in the junior school as children become more self-conscious. Dressing up permits them to act in ways other than those expected and liberates them in ways otherwise forbidden in the curriculum.

The children's responses

The results of the project were diverse and interesting. The first group presented 'Henry this is your life …so far' with Catherine of Aragon as the main protagonist explaining how she was happy to marry Henry and how settled she was, until Anne Boleyn came along.

The second group offered a debate between Anne, Henry and Wolsey over the subject of divorce. Anne was a very forceful character, determined to have things her own way.

Following this episode, Jane Seymour, from the third group, read some poetry Henry had written for her and told everyone how sweet he was. After Jane's death, the storyteller briefly mentioned Anne of Cleves and explained Henry's distaste for the 'Flanders mare'.

The final group began by showing an unfortunate Catherine Howard being dragged off to execution. The class had been learning about medicine men in Henry's time so Catherine Parr quizzed a medicine man about his potions - just before Henry fell off his chair and died.

All the children were fully engaged for over an hour in collaborative work and considerable team effort went into the presentations. They were *participatory* and *reflective* listeners, supporting each other and fully occupied with the task in hand. This group work required a cooperative response and the children's learning was certainly enhanced by working collaboratively (Corden: 2000). The performance was the climax of the lesson but the children were also asked to reflect, briefly, on what they had learnt. Their evaluations produced some interesting answers.

What the children learned about history

Many of the comments illustrated that the children had re-evaluated their opinions about Henry's character. The process of re-enacting his life story challenged the common perception that Henry was a bad-tempered and bloodthirsty monarch, feared by everyone as the children's reflections in Figures 4.0, 4.1, 4.2 and 4.3 show:

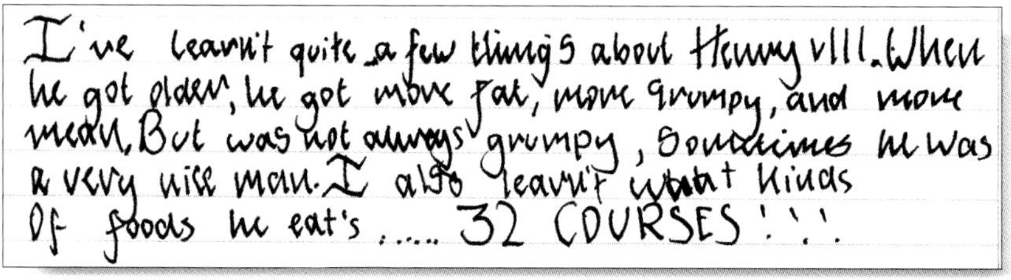

> I've learnt quite a few things about Henry VIII. When he got older, he got more fat, more grumpy, and more mean. But was not always grumpy, Sometimes he was a very nice man. I also learnt what kinds of foods he eat's ..... 32 COURSES!...

Figure 4.0

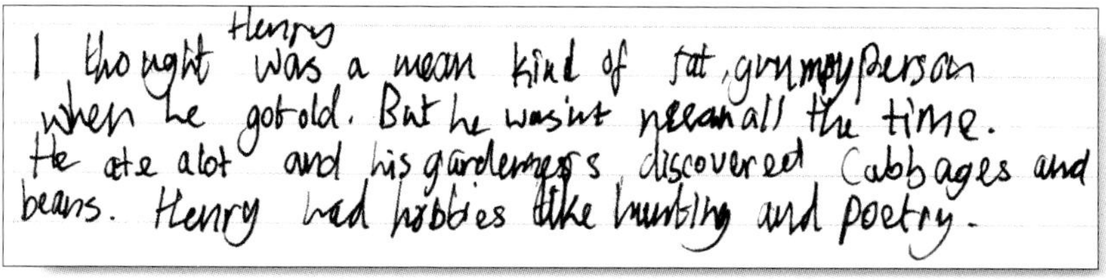

> I thought Henry was a mean kind of fat, grumpy person when he got old. But he wasn't mean all the time. He ate alot and his gardener's discovered cabbages and beans. Henry had hobbies like hunting and poetry.

Figure 4.1

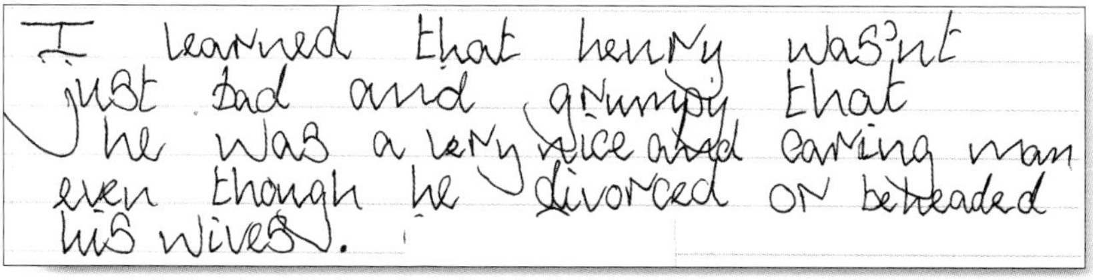

> I learned that henry wasn't just bad and grumpy that he was a very nice and caring man even though he divorced or beheaded his wives.

Figure 4.2

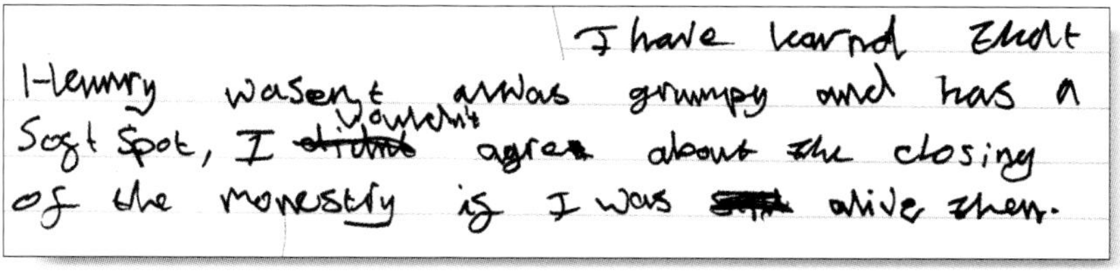

> I have learnt that Henry wasen't always grumpy and has a soft spot, I wouldn't agree about the closing of the monestry is I was alive then.

Figure 4.3

The comments also indicated the extra knowledge that the children had gained from the session (Figures 4.4. and 4.5).

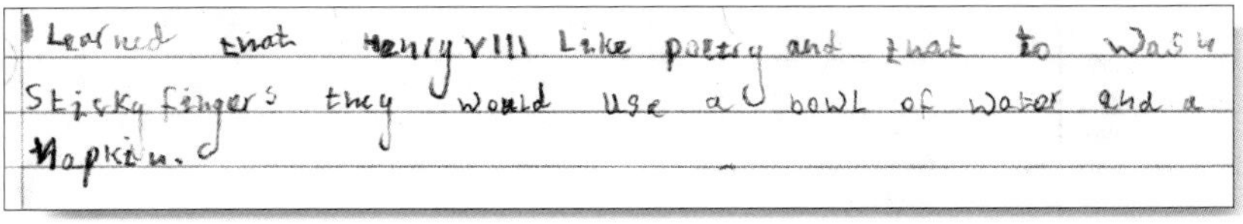

> Learned that Henry VIII Like poetry and that to wash Sticky fingers they would use a bowl of water and a Napkin.

Figure 4.4

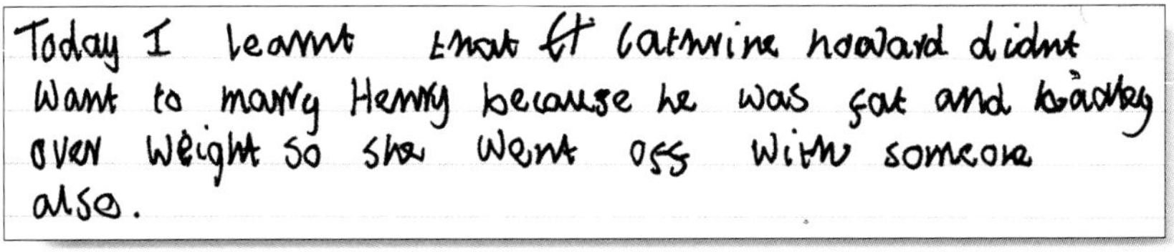

> Today I learnt that ft Catherine howard didnt want to marry Henry because he was fat and backey over weight so she went off with someone also.

Figure 4.5

One child was unsure of the order of the wives but the visual impact of the storytelling had given a more tactile and comprehensive understanding. Figure 4.6 shows that the facts had been demonstrated in a way that was easier to digest and gave a more complete mental picture:

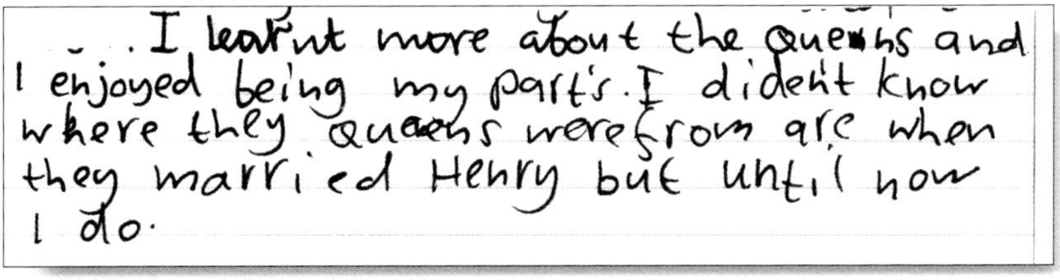

> ...I learnt more about the queens and I enjoyed being my parts. I dident know where they queens were from are when they married Henry but until now I do.

Figure 4.6

Another child engaged with the character and the narrative by relating it to her own experience of family life (Figure 4.7):

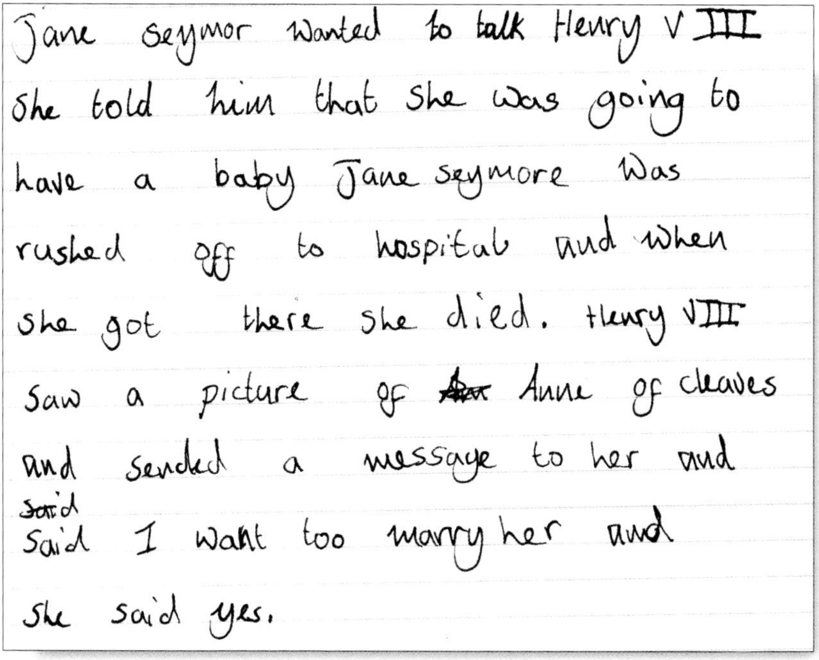

> Jane Seymor wanted to talk Henry VIII She told him that she was going to have a baby Jane Seymore was rushed off to hospital and when she got there she died. Henry VIII saw a picture of Anne of cleaves and sended a message to her and said I want too marry her and she said yes.

Figure 4.7

Even though the final statement shows some historical inaccuracies ('rushed off to hospital') it also demonstrates how the child in question has personalised her learning in a way that makes her unlikely to forget what happened to Jane, Henry or Anne.

All these statements demonstrate how the storytelling/drama had enabled the children to see beyond the facts and bring the characters to life. They show not just chronological awareness, but also knowledge and understanding, interpretation, enquiry, organisation and communication. Instead of facts on a page they had empathised with the living, breathing people behind the scenes and in doing so had deepened their understanding and knowledge of society in the time of the Tudors.

The views of the teachers

Teachers were asked to comment on how they thought storytelling could enhance the curriculum commented:

> *It brings the past to life.*
> *(I use it) to demonstrate how the passing of time distorts history.*

This second comment goes to the very heart of historical enquiry. It demonstrates how our perceptions of 'facts' are influenced by how those facts are presented to us. It has been said that the popularity of the television series *A History of Britain* is due to the storytelling skills of the presenter, Simon Schama (Schama, 2002). Schama himself admits that the strength of the story draws the audience in and engages people's imagination before introducing historical argument.

In the same way, using storytelling to bring characters and events to life for children helps them to develop more understanding of those events and make them more memorable. Discussing, collaborating, enacting and evaluating the learning is more valuable than trying to regurgitate facts and figures in a meaningless context. It also enables children to establish the differences between facts and opinions and to realise that as time passes our 'knowledge' of events is reshaped and changed by our own experiences and attitudes. It encourages children to listen *actively* to each other and to hold meaningful conversations, to use talk to think through the task in hand and to develop comprehension.

Chapter 4

Storytelling and writing

Writing should not always be seen as the end product of storytelling. The enjoyment of the story, the understanding it builds and the oral work involved is just as valuable, if not more so, than written 'evidence'. To give children strong foundations in oral language is essential. The child who has nothing to talk about has nothing to write about (Weir: 2001) so it is imperative that we give children opportunities to listen to stories as often as possible. To listen and talk about personal reactions and experiences based on a story and the questions or images it poses can be a sound and sufficient basis for a literacy lesson. However, sometimes children want to write because the story has given them a purpose for their writing.

Wanting to write in a reception class

Fred the Ted was a travelling bear who had just emailed the children to tell them he had arrived in Dublin and was going to Northern Ireland to visit the Giant's Causeway. I was invited to tell the children the story of the two giants, an Irish legend about the Giant's Causeway. After telling the legend of how the causeway was ripped up and thrown into the sea and the story of the fight between Finn McCool and McConigle, complete with graphic description and bloodthirsty events, I asked the children if they thought they should warn Fred about the giants. The response was immediate and, even though it was last thing in the afternoon, the children wanted some paper to write and warn Fred to look out for the giant. Surprisingly none of the children suggested emailing Fred instead of writing although this would have been an equally effective mode of communication. However, since this project started the use of email in the reception class has increased and the Early Years children are encouraged to use email, as well as letters and postcards, to contact Fred.

Examples from a reception class

Figures 5.0, 5.1, 5.2 and 5.3 were written as warnings to Fred the Ted who was in Ireland.

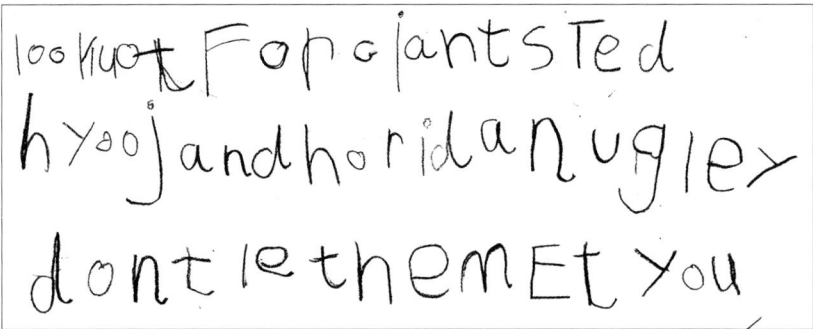

Figure 5.0

Figure 5.1

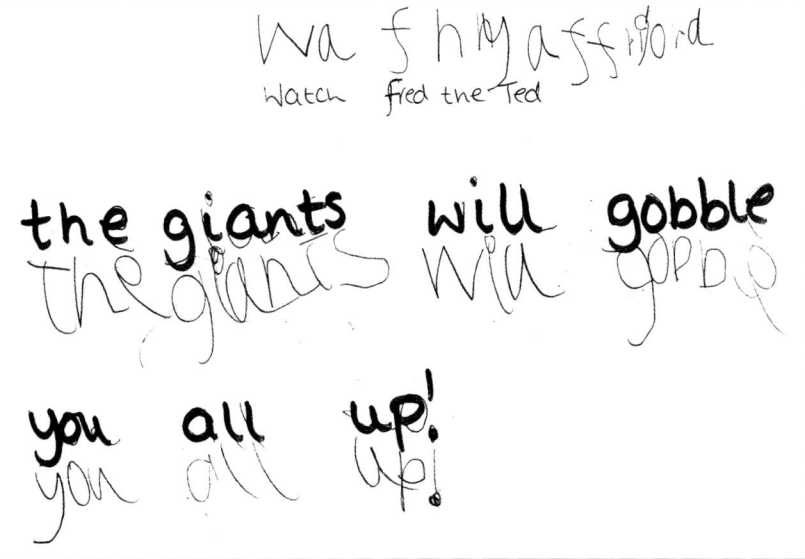

Figure 5.2

Figure 5.3

Personal narrative

Talking is the most natural form of communication and narrative is our way of explaining experiences and central to organising our lives. Personal tales can be developed to aid understanding of story structure. Rosen (1985) regards personal narratives as important, but neglected in classrooms, which is unfortunate as giving children a voice for their problems and anxieties helps release pent up emotions. Maguire (1998) stresses the use of personal stories to connect with and communicate more effectively with others. The pressures of the curriculum mean that there is little time in the school day for children to find their personal voices. 'News-time' used to be a feature in every infant classroom, when children had the chance to share their personal news and views, but it seems this has been largely swallowed up in the need to reach targets in reading and writing. With current interests moving more towards well-being as central to learning, perhaps this may change and children will have more opportunities to be listened to by both adults and their peers.

One way to extend the personal anecdote is by passing on stories based on real-life experiences. Children can pass on a story to a companion who then elaborates on the tale listened to before passing it on to another person - a sort of story chain. By telling personal tales and then passing on those stories with appropriate embellishments we can create different versions of stories. This helps children to understand story structure and come to terms with life events as well as developing the ability to redraft orally. Jones (1988) observed how even young children are able to do this, although the following suggestions are probably more suited to the junior classroom.

Passing on the story

Passing on storytelling encourages creative and imaginative thought as well as talk and problem solving (Harrison 1996) and may be used as a precursor for reading and writing. The structure of the narrative and the use of language are highlighted in this method of working. It encourages confidence in oral literacy and creativity and also emphasises the central part of oral storytelling in the drafting and redrafting of stories before the writing phases. In this way redrafting becomes a pleasure, and teachers and pupils benefit.

This activity requires not just active listening, it also asks the listener to interpret and add to the story. The original story is passed on through several re-workings adding different features with each retelling. The ideas have to be expanded over time, for best results.

Embellishments

1. Description

Teaching children how to embellish their stories is relatively easy. First ask the children, in pairs, to relate a simple story to each other. For example, they tell each other about their journey to school. Each child then takes the story they have just heard and retells it, adding description, to another person. This should result in the subject changing from first to third person.

For example:

> *I walked to school. I came out into the street and along the lane to the main road. Then I crossed at the corner. When I got to the school gate I met my friend.*

becomes:

> *He walked slowly to school. He came out into the quiet street and along the lonely lane to the busy main road. He crossed at the corner with the broken lamp-post. When he got to the school gate he met his best friend.*

When children first start to practise this type of oral re-drafting they do not automatically change into third person narrative so they may need this to be pointed out to them and be given plenty of opportunities to apply their ideas. Giving the children a sample sentence to start should ensure that they understand what is required. If everyone has the same starter they will soon be able to see how even a simple statement can be given depth and interest, depending on the imagination of the teller. For example, 'I went down to the station to catch the nine o'clock bus,' could become, 'Joseph staggered out of the door and ran down the hill just in time to see the nine o'clock bus turn the corner and disappear out of sight.' Or 'Amy strolled down the hill in plenty of time for the nine o'clock bus.' Giving the children different examples like this help them to realise they have complete control over what they do to the sentence.

Description into writing

To transfer this idea into writing requires time and modelling. The teacher demonstrating the scribed versions on the whiteboard helps to highlight how the changes may be made. One way to do this is to take a simple sentence and write it on the board:

I stood up and walked to the door.

The teacher reminds the group that when it is passed on the 'I' will change to either 'he' or 'she' or the name of a person. Discussion about the importance of names is a useful teaching point at this time as different names conjure up different images. When I completed this activity with a Year 6 class the name they decided on was Betty and they were all adamant that this was an elderly lady. Some children even went further and gave details of what she looked like, demonstrating the importance of naming characters appropriately.

Examples are shared with the whole class; the teacher listens and in a shared writing activity demonstrates the changes, working with the class to produce a suitable elaboration, while acknowledging that everyone will have their own version. What the class produces is just one example of what could happen:

Betty slowly hauled herself up to her feet and limped, with the aid of her walking stick, to the dusty cellar door.

Each child then takes the sentence, changes it to third person, adds description to it in the form of names, adverbs and adjectives and produces, orally, to a friend, a more detailed version. Each child then writes down the version they have just heard. It does not have to be a perfect reproduction of the oral version; an approximation will suffice at this stage as the objective is to enable children to see how a simple sentence may be changed by a few additions.

This use of a simple opening sentence, like this, embroidered and extended, is a constructive demonstration of how depth can be added easily to provide a more comprehensive picture that could be the opening scene in a story. Giving the children opportunities to play with simple sentences like this, allowing them time to pass the sentences orally and then scribing the changed version is their introduction to oral redrafting. While listening to someone else interpreting the same sentence they learn what is effective in creating a picture in words. Once they have mastered this orally they will be able write more convincing first drafts.

2. Dialogue

When the children have had practice at working on description the story may be passed on again with another dimension added, possibly **dialogue**. Ask the children how they think dialogue can occur if there is only one character. They should realise that dialogue can be the unspoken thoughts of the character; words spoken aloud or dialogue may also be used to introduce another character. An example, with dialogue added, could be given by the teacher to illustrate how thoughts and speech give an extra dimension to a story:

> *Sam walked slowly to school. 'Monday again,' he thought. 'A whole five days until the weekend.' He came out into the quiet street and along the lonely lane to the busy main road. He crossed at the corner with the broken lamp-post. When he got to the school gate he met his best friend.*
> *'Hello, Hugh. Have you done your maths homework? Can I have a look?'*

Once the children are clear about what they are expected to do they take the story they have just heard and add dialogue before passing it on to the next person. Keeping things simple is the trick at this stage. Restrict the time so that children do not have to remember long tales. Short is sweet when first introducing this type of work as children have to listen very carefully to partners while at the same time thinking about how they are going to change the story by their additions. It also needs to be made clear that changing the story and improvising is a good thing as it shows individual thought and imagination. Children need to realise that once the story has passed their lips it becomes something else. Tracing someone's story and seeing how it changes is an interesting activity, as it can become something entirely different. Giving children the chance to consolidate their skills by practice at each step is better than trying to introduce all the elements at once. In fact, each lesson, or set of lessons, may cover just one of these ways to extend the simple structure presented at the beginning.

Dialogue into writing

Indicating that the dialogue helps to move the action along demonstrates to the children how important this aspect is to the development of the story. Addition of dialogue can change the story plot completely and working with the whole class to illustrate this point by looking at different possibilities is one way to exploit this. Is the main character alone or is someone else with her or him? How will that affect the dialogue? Will the dialogue help the reader to understand what is happening in the story and move the action along? Working with the class the teacher may scribe two separate versions of a sentence with dialogue added:

> *Janice stood up slowly, stretched and yawned before walking hesitantly towards the open door leading to the garage.*
> *'What's that noise?' she asked turning to James, who was reading the newspaper while lounging on the settee.*
> *'What noise?' he asked, peering over his spectacles. 'Probably the cat.'*

or

> *Janice stood up slowly, stretched and yawned before walking hesitantly towards the open door leading to the garage. She stopped and turned her head slowly to the side.*
> *'What's that noise?' she thought. 'It sounds as if someone, or something, is in there.'*

Giving two differing viewpoints like this shows how the story starter can be changed to give contradictory ideas to the reader and enables children to see how the dialogue is central to development of characters and stories. Once again children exchange versions and then scribe the story they have heard. This encourages active listening and the sharing of ideas. Alternatively, once they have exchanged ideas, each child may write a draft of their own idea modified after talking and listening to others.

3. Emotion

Alternatively, or in addition, **emotion** could be included. Asking questions like, 'How do you think the person felt at that time?' opens discussions about which words indicate emotions and helps children to realise that their choice of verbs, or adverbs, can be important.

The first example given:

> *I walked to school. I came out into the street and along the lane to the main road. Then I crossed at the corner. When I got to the school gate I met my friend.*

with all the elements added could end up as:

> *He walked slowly and reluctantly to school. 'Monday again,' he moaned to himself. 'No football until Wednesday.' He was really fed up with everything. He came out into the quiet street and, sighing again, shuffled along the lonely lane to the busy main road. Wary of the traffic, he crossed at the corner with the broken lamp-post. When he got to the tall school gate he met his best friend. 'Hello, Hugh. Have you done your maths homework? Can I have a look?' he said, smiling for the first time that day.*

By this stage the children are usually more aware of what is expected and will readily swap their stories with friends adding the various elements. Through use of this oral redrafting process children become aware of the different devices they can use to make a story more interesting without having to labour over worksheets or several versions of the same story. Other features of language may be highlighted in this process, for example onomatopoeic words, or a dramatic pause, could be added. All the steps, as in the example, do not have to be followed and the order is immaterial.

Emotion into writing

After discussion on how to add this aspect the teacher then gathers ideas and scribes for the class. The opening could be further extended or changed. Even the characters could be changed:

> *James stood up slowly, stretched and yawned. He felt exhausted and sighed at the thought of another three days at the office before the weekend. He stopped, turned his head slowly to the side and listened carefully.*
> *'What's that noise?' he thought. 'It sounds as if someone, or something, is in there.'*
> *Gritting his teeth, he strode purposefully towards the open door of the shed.*

In this version the sentences have also been swapped around and this also indicates to the class that they can change the structure of the story to fit their ideas. At all times the children need to be clear that what the teacher is scribing is simply ideas not the finished version - that is left for each individual. The co-operation and collaboration required for this type of work is of benefit for children in terms of their personal and social development as well as encouraging them to think carefully about how the different elements can change something simple into the setting for an exciting story. The sharing of ideas resulting from the oral work ensures that the children have a pool of shared ideas to work from and encourages them to be more aware of the effect of the choice of words used in their stories.

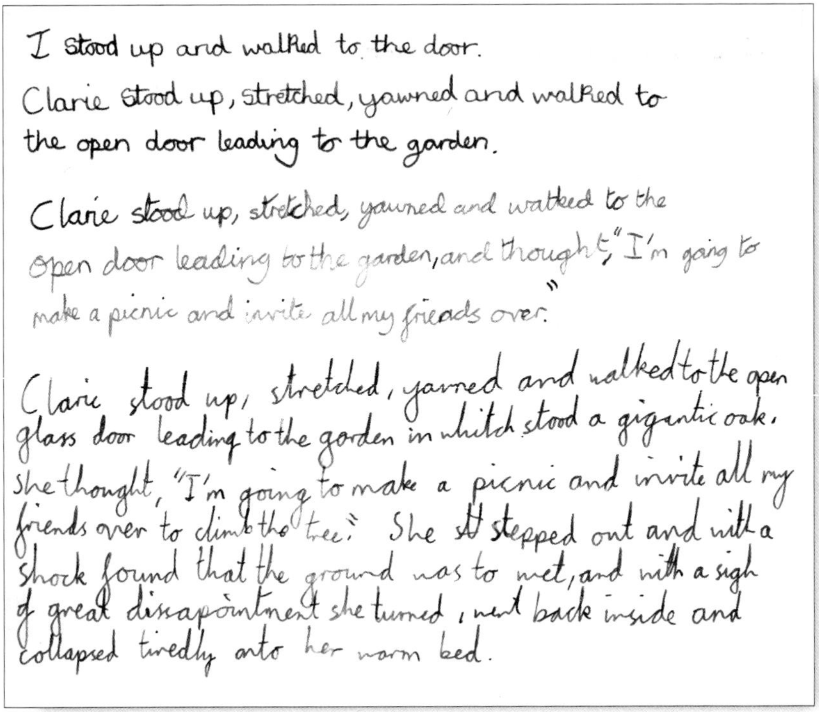

> I stood up and walked to the door.
>
> Clarie stood up, stretched, yawned and walked to the open door leading to the garden.
>
> Clarie stood up, stretched, yawned and walked to the open door leading to the garden, and thought, "I'm going to make a picnic and invite all my friends over."
>
> Clarie stood up, stretched, yawned and walked to the open glass door leading to the garden in which stood a gigantic oak. She thought, "I'm going to make a picnic and invite all my friends over to climb the tree." She st stepped out and with a shock found that the ground was to wet, and with a sigh of great disappointment she turned, went back inside and collapsed tiredly onto her warm bed.

Figure 6.0 Example of work from Year 6

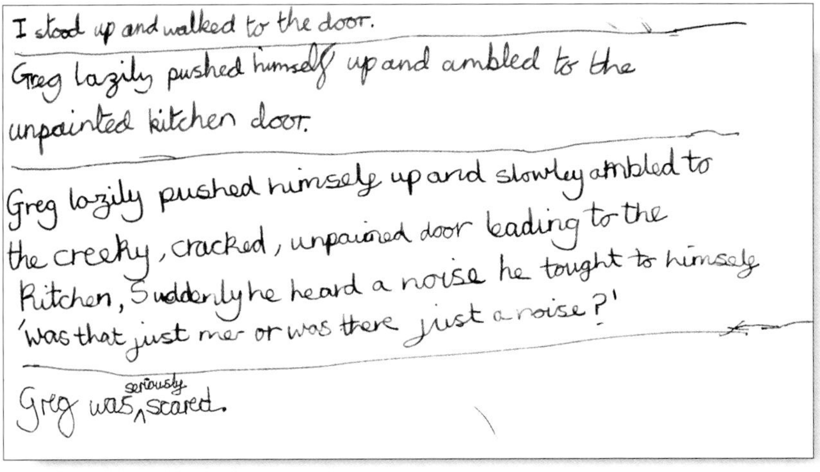

> I stood up and walked to the door.
>
> Greg lazily pushed himself up and ambled to the unpainted kitchen door.
>
> Greg lazily pushed himself up and slowley ambled to the creeky, cracked, unpained door leading to the kitchen, Suddenly he heard a noise he tought to himself 'was that just me or was there just a noise?'
>
> Greg was seriously scared.

Figure 6.0 Example of work from Year 6

Conclusion

Storytelling techniques do not only enhance the speaking and listening skills of children. These methods help change children from superficial, deceptive or even inattentive listeners into more participatory and reflective listeners and learners who may also become more creative thinkers.

Children learn that they can change and adapt ideas easily, that a question may have more than one answer and that stories can be varied to suit the audience. Storytelling introduces them to a variety of vocabulary and thoughts that they can explore as individuals without the fear of being wrong and gives them confidence in their own opinions.

Storytelling may be used to expand understanding of cultural and historical narratives and to develop empathy with other societies. Linked with historical characters it enables children to extend their understanding of the motives behind the actions. It brings the characters to life and also develops the realisation that history is not just facts and figures but an interpretation of those facts.

As a precursor for reading and writing it gives children a firm grounding in the structure and style of story and techniques for improving their own stories (Ralston : 1993). Drafting and redrafting becomes an enjoyable process instead of a slow laborious procedure. If we want the future generation to be effective at all types of communication then we need to nurture their storytelling abilities and encourage them to interact with others. The fact that storytelling is enjoyable as well as educational should be regarded as a bonus rather than something subversive. The word 'fun' does not appear in government guidelines although all good teachers know that to motivate children to want to learn, enthusiasm and enjoyment are key words in the process.

References

Alexander, R. (2002) 'Oracy, Literacy and Pedagogy' Conference Address at *Reaching Out, Moving Forward*: United Kingdom Reading Association International Conference, Chester.

Baker and Greene (1977) *Storytelling Art and Technique*. London : R. R. Bowker.

Bang, J. (2002) 'Time to trash the Three Ts', *The Teacher*. National Union of Teachers: London.

Bearne, E. (2000) Past Perfect and Future Conditional, in G. Cliff Hodges, M.J. Drummond, & M. Styles (Eds.) *Tales, Tellers and Texts*. London: Cassell. 145-156.

Bearne, E., Clark, C., Johnson, A., Manford, P., Mottram, M. and Wolstencroft, H. with Anderson, R. and Gamble, N. (2007) *Reading on Screen Research Report*. Leicester: United Kingdom Literacy Association.

Browne, A. (2007) *Teaching and Learning Communication, Language and Literacy*. London: Paul Chapman Publishing.

Columbia Pictures (2003) *Maid in Manhattan*. Columbia.

Colwell, E. (1980) *Storytelling*. Stroud: Thimble Press.

Corden, R. (2000) *Literacy and Learning Through Talk*. Buckingham: Open University Press.

DfES (2008) *The Primary Framework,* accessed on 12th January 2009 at www.standards.dfes.gov.uk/primaryframework

Fox, C. (1993) *At the Very Edge of the Forest*. London: Cassell.

Gillard, M. (1996) *Storyteller, Storyteacher*. York: Stenhouse Publishers.

Graham, J. and Kelly, A. (2000) *Reading under Control*. (2nd edition) London: David Fulton Publishers.

Grainger, T. (1997) *Traditional Storytelling*. Rugby: Scholastic.

Graves, D. (1990) *Discover Your Own Literacy*. London: Heinemann.

Grugeon, E., and Gardner P., (2000) *The Art of Storytelling for Teachers and Pupils*. London: David Fulton.

Harrison, C. (1996) *The Teaching of Reading: What teachers need to know*. Shepreth, Herts: United Kingdom Reading Association (UKRA).

Howe, A. (1997) *Making Talk Work*. Sheffield: National Association for the Teaching of English (NATE).

Jones, P.(1988) *Lipservice: the story of talk in schools*. Milton Keynes: Open University Press.

Maddern, E. (1993) *The Fire Children*. London: Frances Lincoln.

Maguire, J. (1998) *The Power of Personal Storytelling*. New York: Tarcher/Putnam.

Mallan, K. (1991) *Children as Storytellers*. Newtown, NSW: Primary English Teaching Association.

Meek, M. (1991) *On Being Literate*. London: Bodley Head.

Paley, G.V. (1995) in H. McEwan & K. Egan, (1995) (eds) *Narrative in Teaching, Learning and Research*. New York: Teachers College Press.

Ralston, M. V. (1993) *An Exchange of Gifts. A Storyteller's Handbook*. Markham, Ont: Pippin.

Rose, J. (2008) *The Independent Review of the Primary Curriculum: Interim Report* accessed on 8th January, 2009 on http://publications.teachernet.gov.uk

Rosen, H. (1985) *Stories and Meanings*. Sheffield: National Association for the Teaching of English (NATE).

Rubright, L. (1996) *Beyond the Beanstalk*. Portsmouth, NH: Heinemann.

Schama, S. (2002) *A History of Britain Vols 1 and 2*. London: Ebury Press.

Shaw, S. and Hawes, T. (1998) *Effective Teaching in the Primary Classroom*. Leicester: The Services Ltd.

Turner- Bisset, R. (2001) Serving Maids and Literacy: an approach to teaching literacy through history and music in *Reading*, 35(1):27-31.

United Kingdom Literacy Association/Qualifications and Curriculum Authority (2004) *More than Words: multimodal texts in the classroom* London: QCA. This can be accessed on: http://www.qca.org.uk

United Kingdom Literacy Association/Qualifications and Curriculum Authority (2005) *More than Words 2: Creating stories on page and screen* London: QCA. This can be accessed on: http://www.qca.org.uk

Weir, L. (2001) *Wait Till Ye Hear: Involving children in storytelling*. Presentation at Other Ways of Seeing: Diversity in Language and Literacy. Proceedings of the 12th European Conference on Reading, Dublin: Reading Association of Ireland.

Winston, J. & Tandy, M. (2001) *Beginning Drama*. 2nd edition. London: Fulton

Zipes, J. (2001) *The Oxford Companion to Fairy Tales*. London: Oxford U.P.

Further Reading

Chambers, A.(1984) *Introducing Books to Children*. London: Heinemann.

Clark, M. (1994) *Young Literacy Learners*. Rugby: Scholastic.

Egan, K. (1998) *Teaching as Storytelling*. London : Routledge.

Holderness, J., & Lalljee, B. (1998) (eds) *An Introduction to Oracy*. London: Cassell.

Palmer, S. (2002) 'Pass it on' London : Times Educational Supplement Primary Magazine. June 2nd 2002. London: TES.

Perera, K. (1984) *Children's Writing and Reading*. London: Blackwell.

Smyth, M. (1988) in Weir, L. (1998) *Telling the Tale: A Storytelling Guide*. Birmingham: Youth Libraries Group Library Association.

Resources

What follows is a number of my own personal favourites not mentioned elsewhere in the book. It is by no means a definitive list, merely a list of suggested titles for anyone unsure where to start.

Traditional Tales

The North Wind and the Sun by Brian Wildsmith: (1986) Oxford University Press.
A classic tale retold in simple format. The beautiful illustrations help with memorising the story.

Oh, Kojo! How Could You! By Verna Aardema and Marc Tolon Brown: (1993) Picture Puffins.
An Ashanti tale explaining why cats get better care than dogs. The twists and turns in this traditional tale keep listeners on the edge of their seats.

Monkey Tales by Laurel Dee Gugler illustrated by Vlasta Van Kempen: (1998) Annick Press Ltd.
Retellings of three stories from around the world that stem from the oral tradition. The repetitive refrains encourage children to become involved in the telling.

The Indian Storybook by Rani Singh and Bryan Orion: (1984) Heinemann.
A collection of Indian stories from the oral tradition. The stories are clearly told and suitable for adaptation.

Favourite Fairy Tales by Sarah Hayes, illustrated by P.J. Lynch: (1997) Walker Books.
This collection of twelve stories retold by Sarah Hayes is a classic starter for anyone wanting to use traditional stories in the classroom.

Realms of Gold: Myths and Legends from Around the World by Ann Pilling, illustrated by Kady McDonald Denton: (1993): Kingfisher.
A super collection of familiar and unfamiliar stories from all corners of the globe.

The Princes' Gifts by John Yeoman and Quentin Blake: (1993) Pavilion Books
The nine stories in this book are all based on little known folktales from the oral traditions of many countries.

Tudors and Stuarts

The Six Wives of Henry VIII by Alison Weir : (2000) The Pitkin Biographical Series.
A beautifully illustrated guide to the life and loves of Henry VIII. This guide contains portraits of the wives and extra information about Tudor times.

A History of Britain: The Tudors by Tim Wood: (1990) Ladybird.
An informative guide to life in Tudor times. It covers over a hundred years from Henry VII through to the death of Elizabeth I.

Henry VIII in the series *Famous People, Famous Lives* by Harriet Castor and Peter Kent: (2001) Hachette Children's Books.
A basic, but extremely useful, compilation of information about Henry VIII and life during his reign.

www.history-people.co.uk/
This is the website of a group of people who dress up and re-enact history in classrooms. The website has links to information about characters in Tudor times and provides photographs of people in costume.

www.medievalminstrels.com/Medieval%20and%20Tudor%20music%20on%20CD.htm
This site has resources to buy and free downloads for Tudor and Medieval dance music.

www.headlinehistory.co.uk/online/East%20Midlands/Tudor/eraIndex.htm
Ways to approach history as though through newspaper articles. Information in small bite-sized pieces.

www.thelighthouseforeducation.co.uk/historyks1and2.htm#tudors
Links from this web-site lead to a variety of different resources on Tudor times, including the National Archives.

General

www.storyarts.com
Run by Heather Forest this site has some interesting links and information about storytelling in North America.

www.sfs.org.uk
This is the website for the Society for Storytelling in Britain. As well as information about storytelling in the country and how to find resources it also has link to the storytelling ring - a much larger site with a vast amount of information and stories.

UKLA MINIBOOKS

ALSO AVAILABLE

Minibook 26

Dyslexia and Inclusion: supporting classroom reading with 7-11 year olds

By Rosemary Anderson

What do older primary aged dyslexic pupils do when they are faced with texts at school that are too difficult for them to read independently? The answer, based on findings from the author's research, is that they develop damaging coping strategies and operate on the margins of the classroom community. This book is full of practical advice that will help SENCOs, teachers and assistants to support dyslexic pupils in ways that promote effective learning and ensure inclusion. All the main types of classroom reading encountered are covered, including on-screen texts that are becoming such an integral part of the 21st century school experience.

About the Author

Originally trained as an infant teacher, Rosemary Anderson became a dyslexia specialist in the mid 1990s and then worked as a literacy support teacher until 2007. While studying for the M.Ed. in Literacy at the University of Sheffield, she developed a research interest in the classroom reading experiences of dyslexic pupils during the middle years of schooling, and she recently completed her PhD on this subject. Rosemary now concentrates on freelance writing and works as a volunteer with the RSVP Yorkshire 'Reading in Schools' project.

Minibooks are available from
UKLA Publications, 4th Floor, Attenborough Building, University of Leicester, Leicester LE1 7RH.

UKLA MINIBOOKS

ALSO AVAILABLE

Minibook 27
Practical Bilingual Strategies for Multilingual Classrooms
By Tözün Issa and Alayne Öztürk

One of the challenges faced by Early Years and Primary teachers today is catering effectively for the variety of needs within their classrooms and settings. It can indeed be very challenging to provide appropriate and stimulating activities to facilitate access to the curriculum for bilingual children. The primary aim of this book is to provide some guidance for practitioners through tried and tested strategies to support bilingual learners in the appropriate Key Stages. Suggested activities reflect children's various linguistic and cultural experiences and highlight the importance of maintaining the role of the home language. The practical examples shown in this book reflect positive practice observed both at home and in some schools where such experiences are used most effectively.

About the Authors

Tözün Issa was a classroom teacher for twelve years, and an EMAG Consultant for six years in the boroughs of Tower Hamlets and Lambeth. He completed a PhD on the subject of bilingual education and is currently a lecturer at London Metropolitan University, with a specialism in bilingual education. He is the Director of the Centre for Multilingualism in Education, based at the University.

Alayne Öztürk was a primary classroom teacher for nine years, and she taught English as an Additional Language in Turkey for two years. She is currently Primary Programme Director for Initial Teacher Education at London Metropolitan University. She specialises in literacy education, and is an executive member of the Centre for Multilingualism in Education, based at the university.

Minibooks are available from
UKLA Publications, 4th Floor, Attenborough Building, University of Leicester, Leicester LE1 7RH.

UKLA Minibook Series

Minibooks now no longer in print

Genres in the Classroom	Alison B. Littlefair
Running Family Reading Groups	Sue Beverton, Ann Stuart, Morag Hunter-Carsch and Cecelia Oberist
Teaching Handwriting	Peter Smith
Teaching Spelling	Brigid Smith
Supporting Struggling Readers	Diana Bentley and Dee Reid
Phonological Awareness	Frances James
Exploring the Writing of Genres	Beverley Derewianka
The Power of Words: Guidelines for improving spelling and vocabulary	Norma Mudd
Reading to Find Out	Helen Arnold
Moving Towards Literacy with Environmental Print	Linda Miller
English as an Additional Language: Language and literacy development	Constant Leung